Maths Homework for Key Stage 2

GW01418261

The Active Homework series is a unique collection of practical worksheets, providing 'pencil-free', hands-on activities for English, maths and science, which teachers can use as extension activities in the classroom, or give to pupils as homework to do with members of their family or friends. Practical tasks and discussions form the basis for effective learning, with children and their families learning together.

Each book in the series contains practical activities, utilising everyday resources, which align with the National Curriculum, and the relevant National Strategy documents or QCA schemes of work.

Available titles

Science Homework for Key Stage 2
Colin Forster, Vicki Parfitt, Andrea McGowan and illustrated by David Brookes

English Homework for Key Stage 2
Andrea McGowan, Vicki Parfitt, Colin Forster and illustrated by David Brookes

Maths Homework for Key Stage 2

Activity-based learning

Vicki Parfitt, Colin Forster and Andrea McGowan

Illustrated by David Brookes

This first edition published 2011
by Routledge
2 Park Square, Milton Park, Abingdon, Oxon OX14 4RN

Simultaneously published in the USA and Canada
by Routledge
270 Madison Avenue, New York, NY 10016

Routledge is an imprint of the Taylor & Francis Group, an informa business

© 2011 Vicki Parfitt, Colin Forster and Andrea McGowan for all text. Illustrations © 2011 David Brookes.

Typeset in Frutiger by Wearset Ltd
Printed and bound in Great Britain by MPG Books Group, UK

All rights reserved. No part of this book may be reprinted or reproduced or utilised in any form or by any electronic, mechanical, or other means, now known or hereafter invented, including photocopying and recording, or in any information storage or retrieval system, without permission in writing from the publishers.

The right of Vicki Parfitt, Colin Forster and Andrea McGowan as authors with David Brookes as illustrator of this work has been asserted by him/her in accordance with sections 77 and 78 of the Copyright, Designs and Patents Act 1988.

British Library Cataloguing in Publication Data
A catalogue record for this book is available from the British Library

Library of Congress Cataloging-in-Publication Data
Parfitt, Vicki.
Maths homework for key stage 2: activity-based learning/by Vicki Parfitt, Colin Forster and Andrea McGowan; illustrated by David Brookes.
p. cm.
1. Mathematics–Study and teaching (Elementary)–Activity programs–Great Britain. 2. Homework–Great Britain. 3. Education, Elementary–Parent participation–Great Britain. 4. Active learning–Great Britain. I. Forster, Colin. II. McGowan, Andrea. III. Title. IV. Title: Maths homework for key stage two.

QA135.6.P35 2011
372.7–dc22

2010013209

ISBN10: 0-415-49625-X (pbk)
ISBN10: 0-203-84231-6 (ebk)
ISBN13: 978-0-415-49625-4 (pbk)
ISBN13: 978-0-203-84231-7 (ebk)

To GB.
Thank you.

Contents

Guidance for the teacher: how to use this 'pencil-free' homework book

Introduction

Many primary school teachers feel frustrated when they find themselves setting homework that they know isn't helping the children with their learning. Maybe the tasks are boring, poorly matched to the children's abilities, and too worksheet oriented. Maybe they know the tasks do nothing to reinforce learning, but instead reinforce negative feelings about learning. Many teachers feel frustrated that setting, collecting and marking homework is a chore with little return in terms of children's learning. Too often homework can become a site of tension between teachers and children and between teachers and parents, not to mention between children and parents, and the home–school partnership is diminished, not strengthened.

Maths Homework for Key Stage 2 is a resource that aims to make homework a more positive experience for all concerned, especially children.

Pedagogy and philosophy

Primary school teachers know that children learn through doing and that talking about their experiences is a crucial part of the learning process, as it enables children to revisit and reinforce ideas by reworking them in their own words. However, for many children, homework has become synonymous with 'doing the worksheet' and for many parents homework is about 'getting the sheet done'.

Maths Homework for Key Stage 2 provides good opportunities for learning through doing and for parents/carers to talk with the children about their ideas to share in the learning. *Maths Homework for Key Stage 2* enables teachers to set homework that they feel is learning-focused, rather than task-focused, and helps foster positive relationships between all members of the school community.

Maths Homework for Key Stage 2: the key ideas

*   *Maths Homework for Key Stage 2* is pencil-free; the homework sheets are not worksheets – there is nothing for the child to 'fill in'.
*   Parents and carers are encouraged to share the homework with the child through activity and discussion (but it doesn't just have to be parents – it could be anyone in the family or household).

- The activities are done with items and materials found in the home and focus on discussion.
- Since there is nothing for the child to fill in on the sheet, there is nothing for the teacher to collect in and mark, but there will be lots to talk about in a follow-up discussion.
- The homeworks are arranged in topics to correspond to the QCA scheme of work.
- There is a blank template for teachers to use to devise their own homework activities to allow for further creativity and development.

Following-up on the homework

Whether you select a homework that follows up on work done in class or that introduces a new idea, it is important to follow it up with a class-based discussion about the homework. It would be valuable to find out how the children got on, what they learnt, whether their parents or carers learnt anything and if they raised any good questions about the topic. In this way, it is clear that homework is not a stand-alone activity, but part of a learning process that combines both home and school experiences.

Possible follow-up activities

- Class discussion, with the children reporting on how they got on, and what they found out.
- Class discussion, with the children sharing any questions they raised while doing the activities.
- Group discussions, with each group deciding the most important things they found out.
- Group discussions, with each group deciding which is their favourite question from the ones they all raised.
- Group presentation based on their homework.

Partnership with parents

It is important to keep parents informed of the purpose of the homework and their role in their children's learning. We have provided a draft letter that might be used each term to remind them of the approach taken in *Maths Homework for Key Stage 2*. You may like to use a home–school book for parents to provide some feedback on how they and their children got on with the homework.

Creating your own active homework

We know that our first attempts at creating pencil-free homework will not meet all your needs, so we have included a blank template for you to create your own active homework. We have also provided a selection of icons and pictures that you might use to construct your own tasks.

Template letter

Dear Parent/Carer

Maths homework this term

Our maths topics this term include:

_____

_____

_____

_____

_____

We will be exploring the following ideas:

_____

_____

_____

_____

_____

The maths homework we will be giving on this topic will aim to reinforce these ideas through **doing** and **talking**; we will not be asking the children to fill in a worksheet for their homework as we don't believe this will help them learn.

Why doing and talking? Children learn much more by telling other people about their understanding than they do by being 'told' stuff, and doing active tasks gives them lots to talk about and experiences to reflect on.

It's not just good for children: Parents and carers often don't get to hear much from their children about what they're doing at school, and sharing a discussion is a good way to find out how much your children are learning.

Another advantage: Homework can sometimes become a battleground; we hope children will need less nagging to do this homework and that they, and you, will learn a lot from doing it, and possibly even enjoy some of it.

Feedback to the school: At the bottom of the homework sheet there is space for you to give some feedback to the school on how your child got on with the homework. It would be useful for the school to know if your child grasped the ideas well or explained them clearly, or if they learnt anything from doing the activities. You might also give some feedback on whether they enjoyed the tasks.

How the school will follow up the homework: Your child's teacher will organise a time for the children to discuss and share their experiences of doing the activities. This will give the children the chance to reinforce their learning and for the teacher to assess their progress.

Blank active homework template

Aim of the activity

-
-
-

TRY THIS!

 Think about and discuss

 Ask someone

 Tell someone

Using and applying maths

Patterns and properties: identify properties and patterns of numbers and shapes

Aim

- To identify patterns, relationships and properties involving numbers and shapes.

TRY THIS!

Maths tennis

Read a word from the list to serve and start. Your opposite player then has to return with a maths word that links and is related to yours. If a word is repeated the player is out.

Here's an example:

four – square – shape – sides – vertices – corner – angle – right-angle – 90 – ?

Here are some words to help you start:

divide	double	times	octagon
share	pentagon	weight	volume
add	length	halve	group
increase	difference	decrease	shape

Think of some of your own. All words have to be linked in some way to maths.

Maths Tennis!

FOUR....

SQUARE...

Think about and discuss

Are there any mathematical words that are difficult to link and return?

Solving problems: solving number problems

Aim

- To solve problems involving numbers, money or measures.

TRY THIS!

Number detectives

Choose a number between 1 and 50 and ask a helper to be the detective and ask you questions to find out your number. You can only answer 'Yes' or 'No' to any questions asked.

Some questions to ask could be:

- Is your number bigger than/ smaller than ...?
- Is your number between .... and ....?
- Is your number in the 5-times-table?
- Is your number odd?
- Is your number a multiple of 3?

Swap around and take a turn at guessing the number.

Use measures and money as well as ordinary whole numbers and try larger numbers.

Think about and discuss

Which questions work best when you begin trying to find out the mystery number and which work best towards the end?

Counting and understanding numbers

Recognising number sequences

Aim

- To recognise number sequences formed by counting forwards or backwards in steps of constant size.

TRY THIS!

Hang Five

Ask someone to make up a number sequence of five numbers (e.g. 2, 4, 6, 8, 10 or 15, 17, 19, 21, 23). Your challenge is to guess the sequence before your helper has drawn and hanged the number five in a game on hang-man. Every time you call a number that is not in the sequence a small part of the drawing is added.

A clue can be given by putting one of the numbers into the sequence to start.

Here's an example: _ _ 18 _ _

Answer: 6 12 18 24 30

Move on to sequences of up to eight numbers to make this harder or try sequences of decimal numbers.

Counting on or back in steps of constant size

Aim

- To recognise and continue number sequences formed by counting forwards or backwards in steps of constant size.

TRY THIS!

Count forwards or backwards in a sequence of your choice, missing out one of the numbers.

Ask someone to spot the missing number.

Here are some examples:

6, 12, 18, 30, 36; missing number = 24

4, 7, 10, 16, 19; missing number = 13

Can your helper explain the mistake and correct your number sequence? Swap around so that you get a turn at spotting the mistake.

TRY THIS!

Choose a sound like clapping or finger clicks and decide how much it will be worth.

Cover your eyes while a helper makes the sound. Count the sounds as they clap, and when they stop tell your helper the total value they made.

Here's an example: hand claps will be worth 4. If the number of hand claps made is 6 then the total is 24.

Think about and discuss

Which number sequences do you find hard to follow and count?

Rounding two/three digit numbers to the nearest 10 or 100

Aim

- To round two- or three-digit numbers to the nearest 10 or 100 and give estimates for their sums and differences.

TRY THIS!

? Ask three people you know for their ages. Estimate the total of all three ages by rounding each one to the nearest ten. Explain your estimate to someone else and see if they agree.

TRY THIS!

Estimate the difference between your age and someone else you know. Explain your answer and strategy for working it out to someone else.

? **Ask someone** to check your answer. Would they work out the sum in the same way?

Think about and discuss

Round to the nearest 100 the age of each person in your family. What is the total? What do you notice?

Use decimal notation for tenths and hundredths in real-life settings

Aim

- To use decimal notation for tenths and hundredths in real life settings relating to money and measurement.

TRY THIS!

Estimate the height of someone in your family and tell them the answer only in metres (use a decimal point if needed, e.g. 1.2 metres).

TRY THIS!

Try this with someone: choose other things to estimate and measure, such as your waist, arm length or door height. Do they agree with your estimates? Measure and tell them the answers in metres and centimetres, and in metres only.

Here's an example: 'The width of the book is about 0.2 metres, that's 20 cm.' Measure and find out how close you were.

Ask someone at home for a receipt to look at. Tell them how much each item is worth in pence only.

What fractions (in pence) of £1 do you know? (e.g. 50p is one-half of £1).

Knowing and using number facts

Recall of addition and subtraction facts

Aim

- To know and recall all addition and subtraction facts to 20, sums and differences of multiples of 10 and number pairs that total 100.

Note: number facts or sentences are basic sums (such as $5+5=10$ or $18+2=20$ or $100-50=50$) that are valuable to recall quickly without having to rely on counting procedures.

TRY THIS!

Splat!

Decide on a rule, such as addition facts to 20. Stand back-to-back with a partner and ask a third person to call out a number. The first to say the number that matches to make 20 then turns and 'shoots' to splat their partner.

Here are some rules that you could choose:

- Addition facts to 20
- Addition facts to 100
- Multiples of 10 that make 100
- Multiples of 100 that make 1000
- Multiples of 5 that make 50
- Fractions or decimals that make up 1

Note: a multiple is a number that can be divided by another number without a remainder. For example, multiples of 5 are 5, 10, 15, 20, 25, 30, etc.

Recall of multiplication and division facts

Aim

- To work out and recall multiplication facts, the corresponding division facts and multiples of numbers.

TRY THIS!

Count forwards or backwards in ones from different starting numbers. On a chosen multiple perform an action.

Here are some examples: on multiples of 3, touch your nose, or on multiples of 5, stand on one leg.

To make this trickier, perform the action without saying the number, or try two different rules in the same game.

Think about and discuss

Talk about any numbers where two actions are performed.

Recall of multiplication and division facts

Aim

- To know and recall multiplication facts, the corresponding division facts and the multiples of numbers.

TRY THIS!

Choose a multiplication table and say it while performing one of the following actions:

- Writing your name as many times as you can
- Hopping on one leg
- Clapping a simple rhythm
- Throwing something in the air and catching it

2 times 2 is 4, 2 times 3 is 6...

hop

hop

hop

Think about and discuss

Which multiplication tables do you find most challenging to remember? Tell someone some strategies you could use to help you with the tricky ones.

Using knowledge of addition and subtraction facts

Aim

- To use knowledge of addition and subtraction facts and place value to work out sums and differences of pairs of multiples of 10, 100 or 1000.

Tell someone how if you know a sum like $8 + 2 = 10$ it can help you to know the answers to many more addition and subtraction facts.

Here's an example:

$8 + 2 = 10$	$2 + 8 = 10$	$10 - 2 = 8$
$10 - 8 = 2$	$80 + 20 = 100$	$20 + 80 = 100$

$100 - 20 = 80$	$100 - 80 = 20$	$800 + 200 = 1000$
$200 + 800 = 1000$	$1000 - 800 = 200$	$1000 - 200 = 800$

Here are some more examples to explain:

$6 + 4 = 10$

$10 - 5 = 5$

$3 + 7 = 10$

Think about and discuss

Can you think up some of your own? Does it work for multiplication and division too?

Doubles and halves of two-digit numbers

Aim

- To identify the doubles of two-digit numbers and work out their matching halves.

TRY THIS!

Try this with someone: choose a starting number between 0 and 10 and take it in turns to double it until you reach 100 or more.

Here's an example:

Tell someone what strategies you use to double and halve numbers. Does your helper use any different strategies?

> 2
> 4
> 8
> 16
> 32
> 64

Explain to someone how knowing doubles of two-digit numbers like double 12 or double 16 can help you to know number fact doubles for multiples of 10 and 100.

> 16 + 16 = 32
> so 160 + 160 = 320

> 12 + 12 = 24 so
> 120 +120 = 240 and
> 1200 + 1200 = 2400 !

Tell someone how knowing your number fact doubles can help you to halve 300. What about 5000?

Doubles and halves of two-digit numbers

Aim

- To identify the doubles of two-digit numbers and calculate their matching halves.

TRY THIS!

Choose a starting number from the table below and use the rules to make the target numbers.

The rules are: you can double or halve the number, add 3 or subtract 5 and you can use any combination of these.

Starting numbers	Target numbers
7	20
13	30
42	7
37	10
Choose your own!	

Are you my double?

Erm.... yes and no

Tell someone how your doubles and halves knowledge can help you. What strategies did you use to help you?

Calculations

Use knowledge of number operations to estimate and check calculations

Aim

- To use knowledge of rounding, number operations and inverses to estimate and check calculations.

Note: an inverse is the reverse of a calculation that 'undoes' the effect of the original sum.

For example:

$$2 \times 3 = 6 \qquad 6 \div 2 = 3$$
$$12 + 8 = 20 \qquad 20 - 8 = 12$$

Look at the sums below and explain to someone why they cannot be correct!

Here's an example: $15 \times 5 = 78$

This sum cannot be correct because all numbers when multiplied by 5 end in a 5 or a zero.

$$56 \times 2 = 115 \qquad 150 + 350 = 512 \qquad 56 - 11 = 44$$
$$15 \times 9 = 130 \qquad 19 \times 3 = 58 \qquad 25 \times 5 = 128$$

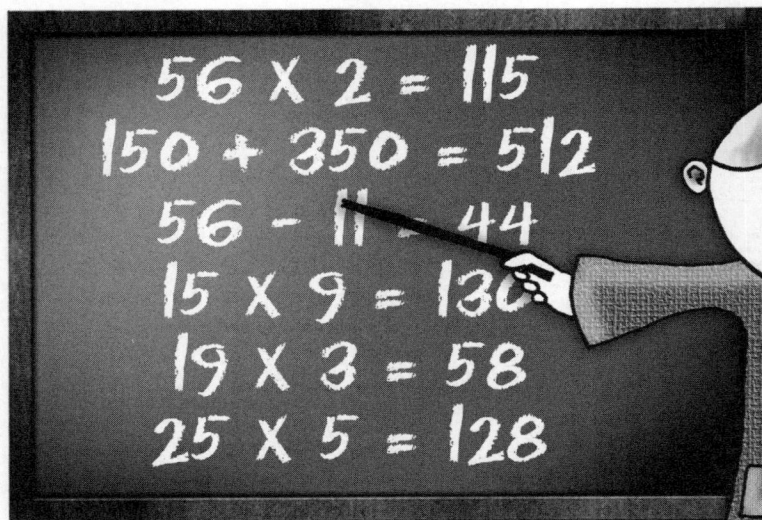

Can you think up some of your own to try on someone else?

Investigate a statement involving numbers and test it with examples

Aim

- To identify and use patterns, relationships and properties of numbers.
- To investigate a statement involving numbers and test it with examples.

TRY THIS!

Investigate the statements below. Using some examples to explain to someone whether they are true or false.

Odd number + odd number = even number

Odd number + even number = even number

Even number + even number = odd number

Odd number × odd number = odd number

Tell someone what other statements you could investigate? Think about statements with division or subtraction.

Solve problems: present and explain solutions

Aim

- To solve problems; present and explain solutions.

TRY THIS!

Pick one of the answers below and, with a helper, each think of a good question that could make the answer using the illustration. Discuss your questions and decide on the best one and why.

37

3 kg

£5.50

125

1 hour 20 mins

> The bus to town leaves at 11:15am and arrives at 11:52am. How many minutes does the journey take?

Solve problems: present and explain solutions

Aim

* To solve problems; present and explain solutions.

Note: (you need a die for this one)

TRY THIS!

Choose a target from the list below. Take it in turns to roll the die and write the number thrown in one of your squares on the grid. Repeat three more times until you have a four-digit number that matches as closely as you can to the target you have chosen. Ask your partner to do the same.

The winner is the person whose number matches most closely to the target.

Targets:

* The largest number
* The number closest to 5000
* A number in the 5-times-table
* The largest multiple of 3
* The smallest even number

Player 1

Player 2

Draw more grids and try rolling your die to make more numbers for different targets.

Tell someone what strategies you are using and how these are helping you to make the numbers.

Make up some of your own targets.

Add or subtract mentally pairs of two-digit whole numbers

Aim

- To add or subtract mentally pairs of two-digit whole numbers.

Tell someone what strategies you use to add and subtract two-digit whole numbers (e.g. 47 + 58, 91 − 34). Explain each of the steps you make.

Here's an example:

Try these:

11 + 12   46 + 34

32 − 12   27 + 45

57 − 45   64 − 35

24 + 35   83 − 38

55 + 35   26 + 26

78 − 44   81 − 37

> For 47 + 58, I add 40 plus 50 to make 90, then add 7+8 together to get 15. So, 90 + 10 + 5 equals 105!

> Or, 50 + 60 equals 110, minus 3, minus 2 equals 105!

Think about and discuss

- Do you add tens or units first? Why?
- Do you use number bonds to 10 or 20? (Here's an example of using number bonds for 55 + 35: when counting the units make a 10 with the 5 + 5.)
- Do you make a picture of the digits in your mind to help you?
- Do you use your knowledge of doubles or halves?
- Do you count forwards or backwards when you are subtracting? Does it depend on the difference between the numbers?

Think about and discuss

Does your helper use the same or some different strategies to you?

Add or subtract mentally pairs of two-digit whole numbers

Aim

- To add or subtract mentally pairs of two-digit whole numbers.

Tell someone what strategies you would use to add/subtract the numbers below. Use examples to describe and explain your methods.

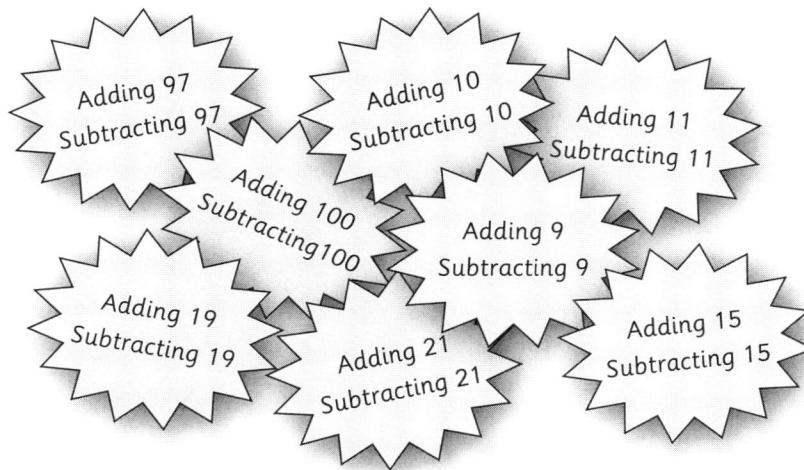

Adding 97
Subtracting 97

Adding 10
Subtracting 10

Adding 11
Subtracting 11

Adding 100
Subtracting 100

Adding 9
Subtracting 9

Adding 19
Subtracting 19

Adding 21
Subtracting 21

Adding 15
Subtracting 15

Think about and discuss

Which of the strategies do you find really tricky? What could you do to get better at them?

Add or subtract mentally combinations of one-digit and two-digit numbers

Aim

- To add or subtract mentally combinations of one-digit and two-digit numbers.

TRY THIS!

Choose any number between 10 and 99 as a target. Take turns to add numbers between 1 and 4 so that you move closer and closer to your target number. The player who hits the target wins the game.

Here's an example: the target number chosen is 25.

Player 1:	4
Player 2:	$4+4=8$
Player 1:	$8+3=11$
Player 2:	$11+4=15$
Player 1:	$15+3=18$
Player 2:	$18+1=19$
Player 1:	$19+1=20$
Player 2:	$20+1=21$
Player 1:	$21+4=25$

PLAYER 1 WINS!

Think about and discuss

What strategies work best?

TRY THIS!

Choose different target numbers or new numbers to add on, such as numbers from 3 to 6.

Use a calculator to carry out calculations

Aim

- To use a calculator to carry out calculations involving all four number operations.

TRY THIS!

Using your calculator, find one way to use all the digits in any order from 1 to 9 to make 100. Try to use all four operations: multiply, divide, add and subtract.

Think about and discuss

How did you decide which operations to use?

TRY THIS!

Find another way to use the same digits to make 100.

Tell someone what you changed and/or kept the same the second time and why.

Carry out one-step and two-step calculations

Aim

- To carry out one-step and two-step calculations involving all four number operations.

Tell someone at home what item you would choose from the menu below.

MENU
Starters
Soup of the Day..........£1.50
Nachos.......................£1.20

Main course
Meat and Gravy........£3.50
Fish, Chips & peas......£4.25
Chicken Salad............£3.75

Dessert
Spotted Dick.............£1.80
Rhubarb Crumble.....£2.05
Jelly and Custard......£1.50

Drinks
Coffee or Tea...............55p
Fruit Smoothie...........40p
Fizzy Pop...................35p

Tell someone how much change you will have from £5.00. What strategy did you use and why? Ask your helper if they would use the same or a different strategy.

Now choose two items to order; how much change from £10.00 will you get?

TRY THIS!

Order different combinations of items and calculate the change from £10.00 each time.

Tell someone how much the nachos and meat and gravy would be if they were half price.

Think about and discuss

Sarah has five coins in her pocket. How much money could she have?

Understanding shape

Use shape vocabulary

Aim

- To visualise, classify and describe shapes and use shape vocabulary.

TRY THIS!

Use the words below to make up at least five sentences that are about 2-D shapes. You can use any combinations of words in any number or order.

Here are some examples:

A **square** has four **equal** sides and four **equal angles**, each **angle** measures 90 **degrees**.

A **regular polygon** has sides of **equal** length.

irregular	sides	area
four	opposite	perimeter
equal	different	square
regular	angle	symmetrical
parallel	rectangle	polygon
degrees	triangle	reflection

Tell someone what sentences you have made.

Are there any words that are tricky to use?

Think about and discuss

What words could you add to the list to make more sentences?

A SQUARE IS A REGULAR SHAPE WITH FOUR EQUAL ANGLES

Describe, visualise and classify shapes

Aim

* To describe, visualise and classify shapes.

TRY THIS!

Choose a 2-D or 3-D shape and ask someone to work out what it is by asking you questions about the properties of your shape. You can only answer 'yes' or 'no' to their questions.

For example:

* Does the shape you are thinking of have more than six faces?
* Does the shape you are thinking of have only straight edges?

Use the shapes below to help you.

square	hexagon
rectangle	polygon
triangle	sphere
circle	cube
isosceles triangle	cuboid
right-angled triangle	cone
scalene triangle	equilateral triangle
parallelogram	cylinder
trapezium	square-based pyramid
pentagon	triangular-based pyramid
rhombus	triangular prism
octagon	hexagonal prism

Think about and discuss

Which questions are best to use at the start of guessing and which work better towards the end? What shape words are most helpful to use?

Describe, visualise and classify shapes: true or false?

> **Aim**
> * To describe, visualise and classify shapes.

Think about and discuss

Look at the statements below and discuss how true they are:

* A square is like a rectangle
* A kite shape is symmetrical
* Only two kinds of 3-D shape will roll
* You can tessellate (make a repeating pattern with no gaps) all 2-D shapes
* Hexagons never have right angles

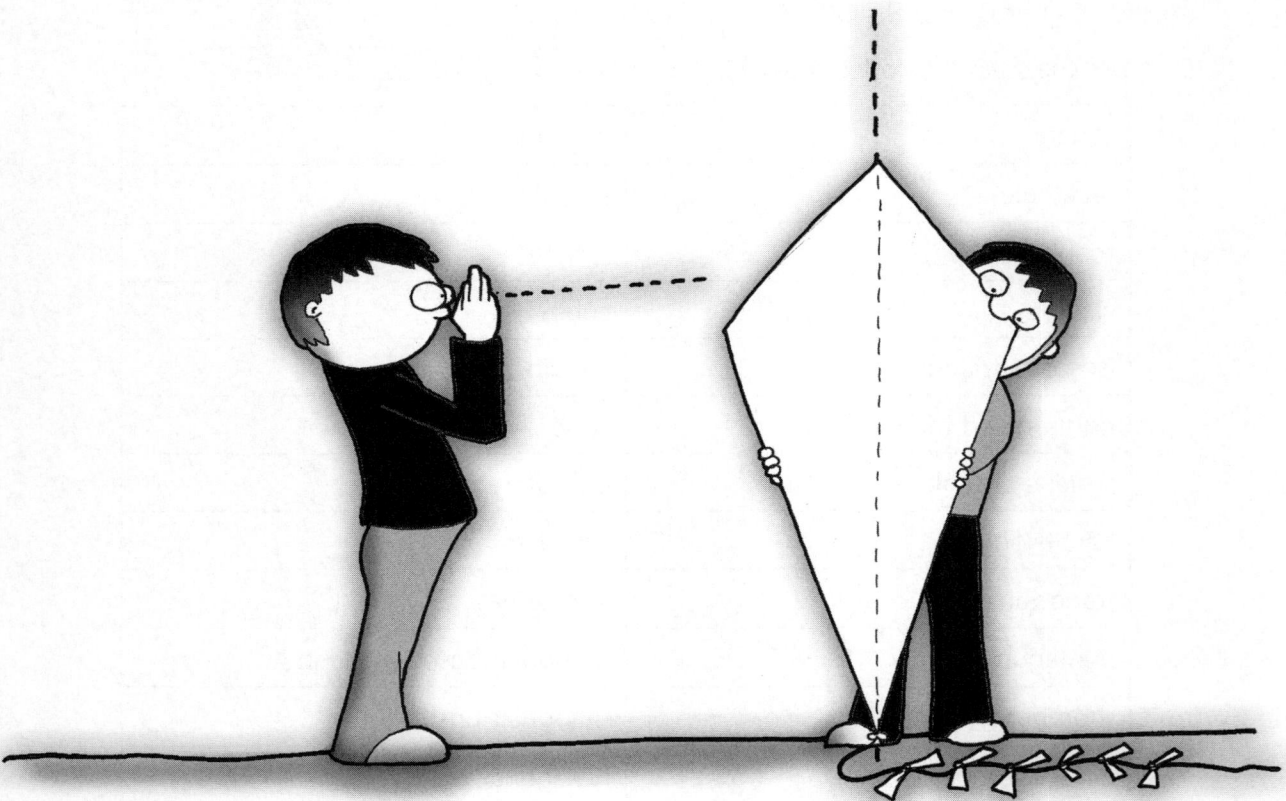

Add some of your own statements to discuss.

Use the vocabulary of position, direction and movement

Aim

* To use the vocabulary of position, direction and movement.

TRY THIS!

Decide where north is (this doesn't have to be the real north). Reac and follow the instructions below and tell someone which compass point you would now be facing.

* Face north. Turn anticlockwise through two right angles.
* Face north. Turn clockwise through two right angles or 180 degrees.
* Face north. Turn clockwise through one right angle.
* Face south. Turn clockwise through one right angle.
* Face south. Turn anticlockwise through three right angles.

Think about and discuss

How many degrees make up a full turn? How many degrees make up half of a quarter-turn?

Use the vocabulary of position, direction and movement

Aim

- To read and use the vocabulary of position, direction and movement.

TRY THIS!

Describe to someone else a route to somewhere you know really well, such as your route to school or to your friend's house.

Use the words below to help you:

Go straight ahead until …	Go past the … then …
Turn left at …	When you get to … turn …
Keep going until …	At the roundabout go …
Turn right at the …	When you get to the traffic lights …

Think about and discuss

Why do maps have grids on them?

Measuring

Choose and use standard metric units

Aim

- To choose and use standard metric units when estimating, measuring and recording length, weight and capacity.

Tell someone what units you would use (e.g. millimetres, centimetres, miles, kilograms) to measure the following:

- Your height
- The area of a football pitch
- The volume of your kitchen sink
- The distance to your school
- The weight of a tree
- The perimeter of your bedroom
- The area of your hand

Think about and discuss

For the units below, what might measure approximately one of each?

- A kilometre (for example, the distance to my school)
- A centimetre
- An hour
- A minute
- A metre
- A kilogram
- A millimetre
- A litre

Choose units of time to measure time intervals

Aim

• To choose units of time to measure time intervals.

TRY THIS!

Estimate first then measure accurately how long it takes to do the activities below. Use your results to calculate the larger amounts and tell someone how you calculated them.

• Estimate then measure how long it takes to hop ten times. Use your result to calculate how long it would take to hop 30 times.

• Estimate then measure how long it takes to write your name. Use your result to calculate how long it would take to write your name four times.

• Estimate then measure how long it takes to say the 5-times-table. Use the result to calculate how long it would take to say the 5-times-table five times.

Think about and discuss

How would you calculate the number of times your heart beats in a minute? Ask someone if they would use the same strategy.

Approximately, how many times does your heart beat in five minutes?

hop

hop

hop

Choose and use standard metric units when estimating weight

Aim

- To choose and use standard metric units when estimating weight.

TRY THIS!

Find items and objects around your home that may be about the same weight. Estimate their weight and use some scales to check how close you were.

Think about and discuss

Which item produced the greatest difference between your estimate and the actual weight? Which items were more challenging to estimate, the lighter or the heavier objects?

TRY THIS!

Find some objects that weigh roughly these amounts:

- 100 g
- 0.5 kg
- 200 g
- 1.2 kg

Calculate time intervals using a calendar

Aim

• To calculate time intervals from clocks and timetables.

TRY THIS!

Find a calendar and use it to think of five questions to ask someone at home. Check to see if their answers are correct.

Here are some examples:

• What day is your birthday on this year?

• How many Mondays are there in December?

• Which months have 30 days?

• What will be the date three weeks from today?

Ask someone to make up five questions to ask you.

Tell someone how you would calculate the number of weeks in a year.

Ask someone if they would use the same strategy.

Extra challenge: how old are you in years, months and days and hours?

Calculate time intervals using a timetable

Aim

- To calculate time intervals from clocks and timetables.

TRY THIS!

Look at the movie guide below, and take it in turns to ask someone a 'time' question about it. Remember to work out the answers and discuss the strategies you both used.

NOW SHOWING

Movie title	Start time	Length
Adventure Kingdom	10:30 am	1 hr 30 mins
Secret Mission 2	12:15 pm	1 hr 45 mins
James Blonde	2:10 pm	2 hrs
Junior School Musical	4:30 pm	1 hr 50 mins
Toy Story 4	6:30 pm	2 hrs 5 mins

Here are some examples:

- At what time does *Secret Mission 2* finish?
- How long do you have to wait for *Junior School Musical* to start after the end of *James Blonde*?
- If *James Blonde* starts ten minutes late, what time will *Junior School Musical* begin?

Think about and discuss

What strategies did you use to work out your answers? Did your helper use the same?

Handling data

Examine and explain the data in a Venn diagram

Aim

- To examine and explain the data in different graphs and charts.

Think about and discuss

The Venn diagram below shows the sports that some people like and dislike. Discuss whether the statements beneath it are true or false.

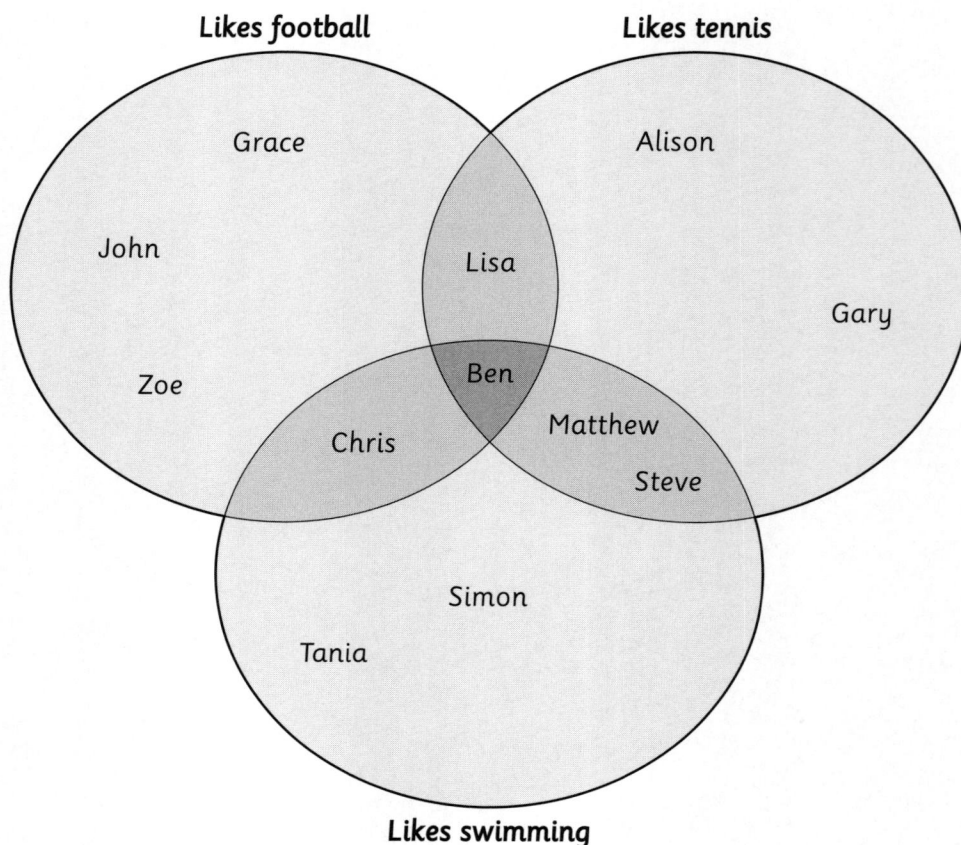

Likes football   **Likes tennis**

Grace

Alison

John

Lisa

Gary

Zoe

Ben

Matthew

Chris

Steve

Simon

Tania

Likes swimming

- Alison doesn't like swimming.
- Five people, in total, like football and tennis.
- Chris likes swimming and football.
- Matthew, Steve and Ben like tennis and football.
- Six people like swimming.
- Lisa likes everything.

Tell someone some statements of your own.

Examine and explain the data in a Carroll diagram

Aim

- To examine and explain the data in different graphs and charts.

Tell someone which numbers in the Carroll diagram below are in the wrong place.

	Numbers in 7-times-table	Numbers not in 7-times-table
Numbers divisible by 3	28 84 56	12 30 23 42
Numbers not divisible by 3	14 21 49 63 7	29 16 15 24

Look out for the pattern...

Think about and discuss

What strategies did you use to work this out? Do you know a quick way to check if numbers belong in the 3-times-table?

Think of some other numbers; where would they go on the grid?

Examine and explain the data in a bar chart

Aim

- To examine and explain the data in different graphs and charts.

Tell someone some facts about the bar chart below.

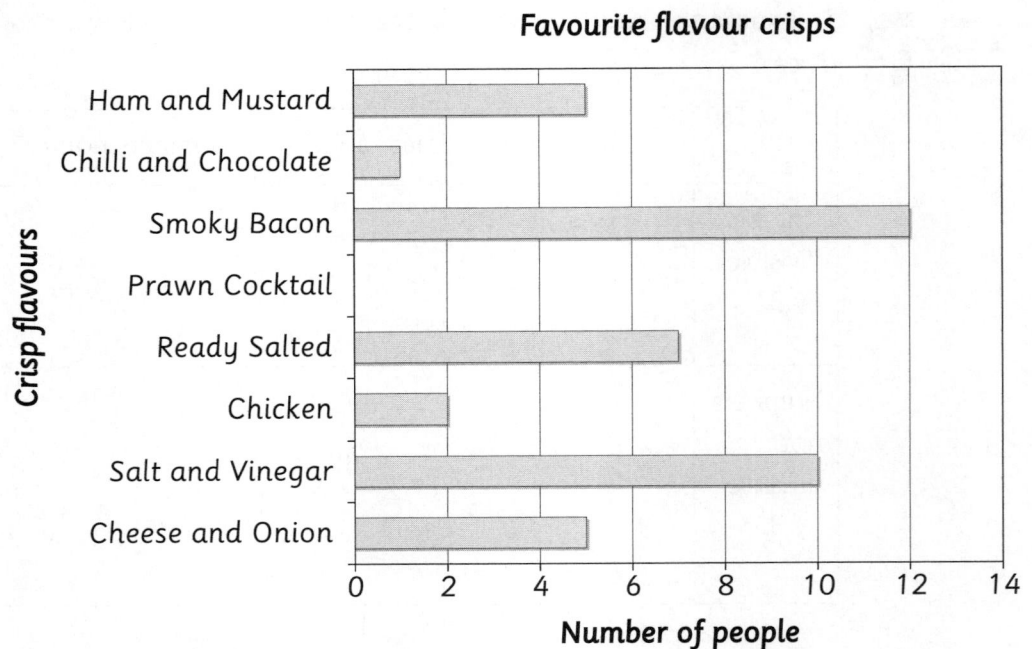

Favourite flavour crisps

Here are some examples:

- The most popular flavour is smoky bacon.
- Seven people prefer ready salted crisps.

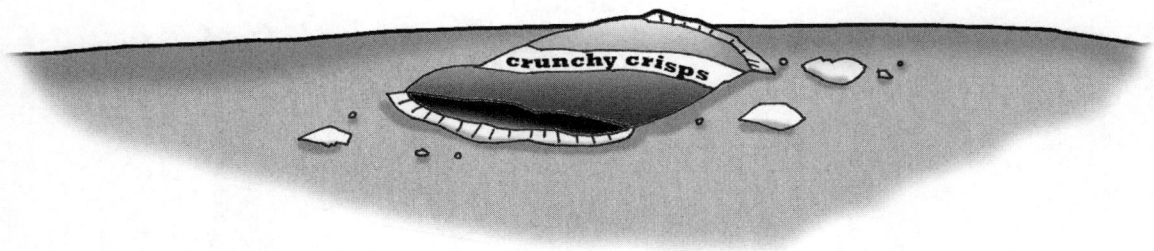

Think about and discuss

How would you calculate the total number of people in the survey? Ask someone if they would use the same strategy as you.

Answer a question by identifying what data to collect and how to organise it

Aim

- To answer a question by identifying what data to collect and how to organise and present it.

Tell someone what data you would need to collect to answer the question below. Explain how you would collect and record your data.

Question: What is the most popular hobby in your class?

Think about and discuss

What information would each axis contain if you presented your results in a bar chart? What size steps might you choose for the number axis? How many bars would your chart need?

Counting and understanding numbers

Finding the difference between positive and negative numbers

Aim

- To find the difference between positive and negative numbers.

TRY THIS!

Think of five pairs of negative numbers with a difference of 16, such as –20 and –4. Ask someone to check your answers and tell them what methods you used to think up the pairs of numbers.

Think about and discuss

The table below shows average temperatures in Celsius for the base camp of Mount Everest and its summit. Use the data to create three questions to ask someone and check to see if they answered correctly.

	Jan	Feb	March	April	May	June
Everest Base Camp	–16	–15	–12	–9	–7	–4
Everest Summit	–36	–34	–33	–30	–24	–18

Here are some examples:

- What is the difference in temperature between the base camp and the summit of Everest in April?
- Which month has the greatest difference in temperature between the base camp and the summit?

Now ask your helper to make up three questions to ask you. Tell them what methods you used to work out the answers.

Extra challenge: what is the difference between 7 and –7? Make up some positive and negative number pairs to calculate the difference.

Counting in whole numbers and decimal steps, extending into negative numbers

Aim

- To count from any given number in whole numbers and decimal steps, extending beyond zero when counting backwards.

TRY THIS!

Count forwards or backwards in a sequence of your choice, missing out one of the numbers. Ask someone to spot the missing number.

Here are some examples:

- 0.7, 0.9, 1.1, 1.5, 1.7, 1.9   missing number = 1.3
- 20, 15, 10, 5, −5, −10   missing number = 0
- 1.2, 1.7, 2.7, 3.2, 3.7, 4.2   missing number = 2.2
- 2.5, 2.25, 1.75, 1.5, 1.25   missing number = 2.0

Can they explain the mistake and correct your number sequence?

Swap around so that you get a turn at spotting the mistake.

Move on to sequences of up to eight numbers to make this harder. Try making sequences that include negative numbers.

Think about and discuss

Which sequences do you find most difficult and why?

Use knowledge and understanding of numbers

Aim

- To use knowledge and understanding of numbers.

TRY THIS!

Ask someone to pick you a number between 1 and 100. Tell them as much about the number as you can. Aim for ten things and use the example below to help you.

Chosen number: 25

- It is an odd number
- Doubling it equals 50
- It is 5 squared
- Half of it equals 12.5
- When it is divided by 3 the answer is 8, remainder 1
- 5 is a factor of it
- It is a multiple of 100
- It is a quarter of 100
- It is ten times bigger than 2.5

are you an odd number?

Well, I've had my moments...

Give your helper a number and challenge them to do the same.

Use bigger numbers or try negative numbers and decimals to make it harder.

Think about and discuss

Which statements were hardest to think up?

Note:

1   A factor is a number that is multiplied to get a quantity (product). For example, 3 and 4 are both factors of 12 and 5 and 3 are factors of 15.
2   A multiple is a number that can be divided by another number without a remainder. For example, multiples of 5 are 5, 10, 15, 20, 25, 30, etc.
3   Square numbers are the result of multiplying a number by itself once. For example, 49 is a square number because $7 \times 7 = 49$.

Calculate fraction sizes

Aim

- To calculate fraction sizes by using the same (common) denominator (the bottom number in a fraction) and relate fractions to decimals.

Think about and discuss

How would you find out which is larger, $\frac{7}{10}$ or $\frac{4}{5}$?

Use > or < to show which fraction is larger.

Here is one method. Find the common denominator (make the number on the bottom of the fraction the same for both fractions).

If you have a different method you could also use this.

Note: Remember that whatever you change on the bottom of the fraction you must also change on the top.

$$\frac{7 \times 2}{10 \times 2} = \frac{14}{20}$$

$$\frac{4 \times 4}{5 \times 4} = \frac{16}{20}$$

So, $\frac{7}{10} < \frac{4}{5}$

$\frac{4}{5}$ is larger than $\frac{7}{10}$

Tell someone which is the larger fraction. Explain how you worked out the common denominator.

$\frac{5}{6}$ or $\frac{6}{8}$

$\frac{2}{3}$ or $\frac{5}{8}$

$\frac{7}{8}$ or $\frac{4}{5}$

Think about and discuss

Would changing the fractions to decimals be a good method? Could you use a calculator to help you?

Relate and convert fractions to specific quantities

Aim

- To relate and convert fractions to specific quantities.

Think about and discuss

Are the statements below true or false?

- $\frac{1}{10}$ of a pound is 1p.

- $\frac{1}{10}$ of a kilogram is 100 g.

- $\frac{4}{10}$ of 1 m is 400 cm.

- $\frac{5}{100}$ of a metre is 5 cm.

- $\frac{2}{1000}$ of 1 kg is 20 g.

Explain your answers to someone and see if they agree.

TRY THIS!

Think of some statements of your own to try out on someone.

Think about and discuss

If the month of February (28 days) is the whole, what fraction is one week? What about one day?

Count in whole numbers and decimal steps

Aim

- To count from given numbers in whole numbers and decimal steps.

TRY THIS!

Pick a starting number that is less than 2 and to one decimal place (e.g. 1.2, 0.7, 1.9). Ask someone to pick a target number between 10 and 30.

Take it in turns to double the starting number. The winner is the first person to say a number above the target number and scores one point. Repeat the game until someone reaches three points.

Here is an example:

- Start number 1.2
- Target number 15
- 1.2, 2.4, 4.8, 9.6, 19.2 – Player 1 is the winner!

Think about and discuss

What strategies do you use to double the decimals?

Extra challenge: to make this harder make the starting number between 2 and 4 and the target number between 20 and 50.

Understand and order decimals

Aim

* To understand and order decimals with tenths, hundredths and thousandths.

TRY THIS!

Choose two decimal numbers from the table below and tell someone which is the bigger number.

0.45	0.5	0.48	0.51	0.53
0.4	4.3	4.53	4.31	4.5
4.45	5.5	4.45	5.75	5.5
0.55	0.54	5.05	0.04	4.05
0.05	4.03	4.35	5.35	5.4

Here's an example:

0.5 is larger than 0.04 because five-tenths of something is more than four-hundredths.

To make this harder try finding the difference between each pair of numbers that you choose or find the total of each pair.

Tell someone what the value of each of these digits is: 5.874.

Think about and discuss

What happens if you move the decimal point on this number one place to the right?

Solve problems involving proportions and quantities

Aim

- To solve problems involving proportions and quantities by scaling quantities up or down.

TRY THIS!

The recipe below makes about 30 blueberry muffins. Calculate how much of each ingredient is needed to make 90 muffins. Tell someone your measures and explain the methods you used.

Ask them to check your answers. Would they use the same strategies?

Blueberry muffins

3 eggs
125 g soft brown sugar
100 g caster sugar
500 ml milk
125 ml sunflower oil
300 g plain four
160 g wholemeal plain flour
$\frac{1}{2}$ tsp salt
25 g bran
175 g fresh blueberries
2 tsp bicarbonate of soda

Think about and discuss

If you only wanted to make 15 muffins, scale down the quantities to calculate how much of each ingredient you would need.

Knowing and using number facts

Use number knowledge to estimate and check calculations

Aim

- To use knowledge of number facts, place value and the inverse function to estimate and check calculations.

Think about and discuss

Read the statements below and discuss each one. Think of at least three examples to check each statement.

- A number that is exactly divisible by 9 is also exactly divisible by 3.
- A number that is exactly divisible by 6 is also exactly divisible by 3.
- If the sum of a number's digits is divisible by 3 the number is a multiple of 3.
- A number is divisible by 4 if the number's last two digits are divisible by 4.
- Halve and halve again – if the answer is even the original number is a multiple of 8.

$$18 \div 9 = 2$$
$$18 \div 3 = 6$$

Can you think of some of your own to test on someone?

Note: an inverse is the reverse of a calculation that 'undoes' the effect of the original sum. For example, if $2 \times 3 = 6$, then $6 \div 2 = 3$.

Use knowledge of multiplication and division to solve calculations

Aim

- To use knowledge of place value and multiplication facts and the inverse function to solve calculations.

Think about and discuss

Look at the sums in the box below and use one of them each time to solve the calculations beneath. Explain your answers to someone and tell them how you used the sums to help you.

$6 \times 8 = 48$
$56 \div 7 = 8$
$23 \times 25 = 575$
$72 \div 9 = 8$

What is 60×8?
What is 230×250?
What is 23×26?
What is $575 \div 23$?
What is $7.2 \div 9$?
What is 2.3×2.5?
What is $720 \div 9$?

Make up some calculations of your own that can be solved using the sums above. Ask someone to solve them.

Identifying factors and multiples

Aim

- To identify pairs of factors of two-digit whole numbers and find common multiples.

Note: a factor is a number that is multiplied by another to get a quantity (product). For example, 3 and 4 are factors of 12; 5 and 3 are factors of 15.

Tell someone pairs of factors for the numbers in the stars below.

72   64   32   56
    48   35
36   81   54
        72   42   16
24   40

TRY THIS!

Work with someone else to find other ways of reaching these numbers using more than two factors each time.

Here's an example: $36 = 3 \times 3 \times 2 \times 2$ (these are called prime factors).

PLEASE QUEUE HERE

2 3 5 7 11

Use knowledge of factors and multiples to solve problems

Aim

- To use knowledge of factors and multiples to solve problems.

Think about and discuss

Look at the statements below and decide whether they are true or false. Explain your answer and see if someone else agrees with your results.

- 8 is a multiple of 2
- 7 has only two factors
- 6 is a factor of 20
- 64 has only one pair of factors
- 24 has five pairs of factors
- All multiples of 5 are odd numbers
- There are eight prime numbers between 1 and 20
- There are 11 prime numbers between 50 and 100

> **Remember that a factor is a number that is multiplied to get a quantity (product). E.g. 3 and 4 are both factors of 12 and 5 and 3 are factors of 15.**

Make up some of your own true-or-false statements and test them out on someone else.

Think about and discuss

What is the difference between a factor and a multiple? Why isn't 1 a prime number? What is the only even prime number?

Use knowledge of multiplication facts to calculate squares of numbers

Aim

- To use knowledge of multiplication facts to calculate squares of numbers.

Note: a square number is the product of a whole number multiplied by itself. For example, $5 \times 5 = 25$, so 25 is a square number.

Tell someone all the square numbers up to 100, starting with 1×1, then 2×2, and so on.

TRY THIS!

Ask someone to choose a target number between 1 and 100. Reach the target number by using one or more square numbers and either an addition or a subtraction.

Here are some examples:

- Target number is $47 = 6 \times 6 + 11$
- Target number is $61 = 8 \times 8 - 3$

> **Remember that a square number is the result of multiplying a number by itself once. E.g. 49 is a square number because 7x7=49**

Swap over and choose a target number for someone else to hit.

Think about and discuss

Talk about the strategies that you use and which work best.

To make this harder try numbers greater than 100.

Here's an example:
Target number is $160 = (10 \times 11) + (7 \times 7) + 1$

Use approximations, inverse operations to estimate and check results

Aim

- To use approximations, inverse operations and tests of divisibility to estimate and check results.

Think about and discuss

Look at the numbers below and talk about whether you would estimate them to the nearest 10, 100, 1000, 10,000, 100,000 or 1,000,000. Compare and discuss your answers.

- Words in a dictionary
- People in your nearest town
- Baked beans in a tin
- Fans at a football match
- Children in your school
- Books in your school library
- Your height in hand spans

Think up your own to ask someone

Estimate the answers to the questions below and tell someone. Explain how you would check to see how close your estimates are.

- How many times your heart beats in an hour.
- How many 10p coins would make a straight line 1 m long.
- How many words are on a page of your favourite book.
- How many hand spans make up the perimeter of your bedroom.

Set an estimation challenge for someone else.

Calculations

Extend mental methods for number calculations

Aim

- To extend mental methods for number calculations.

TRY THIS!

Write down the following five numbers:

- Your age
- The number of the month your birthday is in, for example write '4' for April
- The first number in your postcode
- The total number of letters in your first name and surname
- The number of letters in the name of the road where you live

Ask someone to give you a target number between 1 and 100. Use any combination of the numbers you have written down along with any operation to calculate mentally the target number. How close can you get?

Think about and discuss

What strategies did you use to help you hit the target number?

To make this harder, make your target numbers greater than 100 or include negative numbers.

Think about and discuss

How would you calculate how old you are in days? Ask someone if they would use the same methods.

Extend mental methods for doubling and halving

Aim

- To extend mental methods for doubling and halving.

TRY THIS!

Choose a starting number from the table below and take it in turns with someone to halve it. The winner is the person to reach the target number.

Start number	Target
96	1.5
64	0.25
72	2.25
112	1.75

TRY THIS!

Choose a starting number from the table below and take it in turns with someone to double it. The winner is the first person to reach 1000 or more.

Start number
125
130
212
78

Think about and discuss

Which strategies work best for you?

Extend mental methods for number calculations

Aim

- To extend mental methods for number calculations.

TRY THIS!

Choose two numbers from the bubbles below and ask someone to double the first number and add it to the second number. Ask them to explain the strategies they used. Have a turn and explain your own methods. Try different numbers.

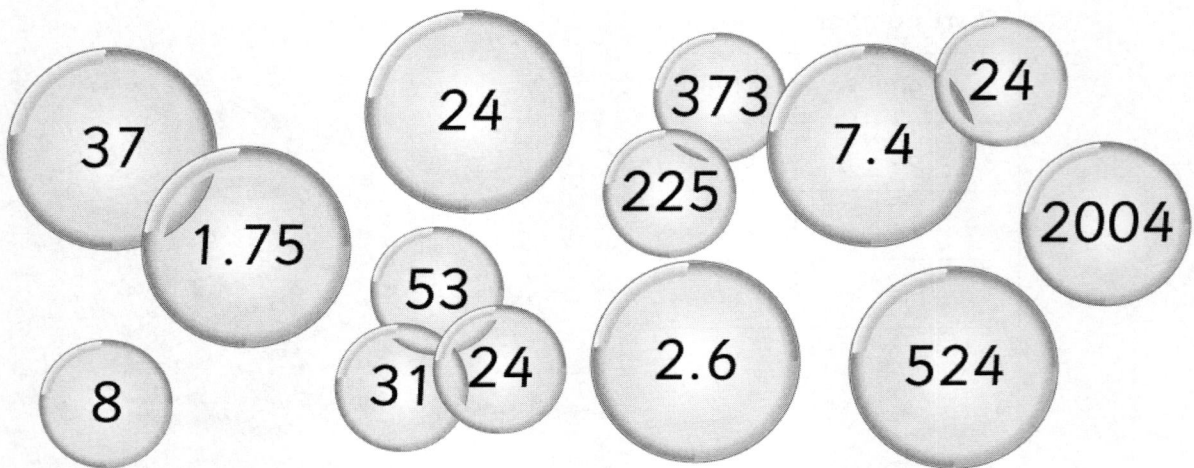

37   24   373   24
1.75   225   7.4
53   2004
8   31 24   2.6   524

Here's an example:

- Chosen numbers: 53 and 524
- $53 \times 2 = 106$ (double 50 then double 3)
- $106 + 524 = 630$ ($500 + 100 = 600$, then $24 + 6 = 30$)

Extend mental methods using all four number operations

Aim

- To extend mental methods using all four number operations.

TRY THIS!

Choose four numbers between 1 and 9 and use any combination of operations to make the target numbers below. Explain your answer to someone.

12, 39, 58, 62, 83

Here's an example:

- Numbers chosen: 2, 3, 5, 7
- Target number: 39
- $3 \times 7 = 21$
- $21 \times 2 = 42$
- $42 - 3 = 39$

Think about and discuss

What strategies worked best for you?

Find fractions and percentages of whole-number quantities

Aim

- To find fractions and percentages of whole-number quantities.

Tell someone how to calculate 10% of a number. What about 25% of a number? Use examples in your explanation.

Ask someone to tell you how s/he would calculate 60% and 90% of a number. Would you use the same methods?

TRY THIS!

Look at the prices of sports equipment below. Calculate the new prices for each item if there was a sale and the items were reduced by 20%. Share the strategies that work for you and find out if others would use the same or different methods.

Hockey stick
£24.00

Tennis racquet
£32.00

Bike
£260.00

Netball
£12.00

£260

To make this harder try reducing each price by 15%.

Extend mental methods for number operations

Aim

- To extend mental methods for number operations.

Think about and discuss

Look at the sums below and talk about why they cannot be correct. Tell someone and see if they agree with you.

- $23 \div 10 = 0.23$
- $1.4 \times 100 = 1400$
- $6070 - 5082 = 1088$
- $16 \times 25 = 500$
- $\frac{1}{10}$ of $5\,kg = 50\,g$

> **The sum is incorrect because the decimal point has moved too far. Do you agree?**

Can you think up some sums of your of your own to test on someone else?

Understanding shape

Identify, visualise and describe properties of shape: shape sentences

Aim

- To identify, visualise and describe properties of shapes.

TRY THIS!

Use the words below to make up at least five sentences. You can use any combinations of words and in any number or order.

angle	equal	area
obtuse	acute	perimeter
protractor	equilateral	parallelogram
right-angle	kite	symmetrical
shape	isosceles	rectangle
degrees	reflex	opposite
equal	trapezium	rhombus
perpendicular	quadrilateral	parallel

Here's an example: a trapezium is a quadrilateral that has one pair of opposite parallel sides.

A *protractor* is used to measure *angles* in *degrees*.

Tell someone the sentences you have made and ask them to make some. Are there any words that are tricky to use?

Think about and discuss

What words could you add to the list to make more sentences?

Identify, visualise and describe properties of shape: describing and guessing

Aim

- To identify, visualise and describe properties of shapes.

TRY THIS!

Pick a shape from the selection below and describe it for someone to guess.

Ask someone to give clues for you to have a turn at guessing.

To make this harder say the number of clues you will try to guess the shape in!

Identify, visualise and describe properties of shape: agree or disagree

Aim

- To identify, visualise and describe properties of shapes.

Think about and discuss

Look at the statements below and discuss whether they can be correct.

- Isosceles triangles never have lines of symmetry.
- All equilateral triangles have three lines of symmetry.
- The same triangle can be scalene and isosceles.
- A cube has 18 edges.
- A cuboid has some parallel edges and some perpendicular edges.
- A cone has no vertices.
- A square-based pyramid has parallel faces.

Tell someone some statements of your own. Can they say if they are correct?

Identify, visualise and describe nets of shape

Aim

- To identify, visualise and describe properties of shapes.

TRY THIS!

Choose a 3-D shape from the list below and describe to someone what its net might look like. Can they name your shape?

Here's an example:

My shape has a net with two squares and four rectangles. What shape is it?

Cube	square-based pyramid
Cuboid	triangle-based pyramid
Cylinder	pentagonal-based pyramid
triangular prism	rhombus prism

My shape has a net with 2 squares and 4 rectangles. What shape is it?

Think about and discuss

How would you calculate the area of the net of a cuboid?

Describing and drawing 2-D shapes

Aim

- To identify, visualise and describe properties of shapes.

TRY THIS!

Find a pencil, ruler and some scrap paper. Choose a 2-D shape and describe it so that someone else is able to make a sketch of it. Do not look at their sketch until you have given all the clues.

Here's an example:

- Draw 4 cm down the page.
- From the bottom of the first line, draw 2 cm to the right so that you have a right angle.
- From the end of the second line, draw a second 4 cm line back up the page so that it is parallel with the first.
- Join the three lines with another 2 cm line.

Swap over and have a go at drawing while someone gives you the clues.

Remember, your shapes do not need to be regular.

Measuring

Estimate and measure length

Aim

• To estimate and measure length with some accuracy.

TRY THIS!

Estimate the area of the smallest room in your house. Tell someone your estimate, then measure to see how close you were. If you do not have a measuring tool you could measure using your feet (one foot is approximately 30 cm).

TRY THIS!

Repeat for the largest room in your house then calculate the difference in area between the two rooms.

Think about and discuss

How might you find the area of shapes that do not have straight sides? Tell someone using examples such as a leaf or a puddle. Find out if they would use the same strategy.

Think about and discuss

How might you calculate the perimeter of your house? Tell someone and find out if they would use the same strategy.

Solving problems with measures

Aim

- To represent a puzzle or problem using statements, sentences cr diagrams; use these to solve the problem and present and interpret the solution.

TRY THIS!

Look at the conversions below and think of three good questions to ask someone. Discuss their answers and the strategies they used.

- 1 pint = 568 ml
- 1 tsp = 5 ml
- 1 kg = 2.2 lbs
- 1 cup = 280 ml
- 5 miles = 8.05 km

Here are some examples:

- About how many cups of tea would fit in a 1-litre flask?
- The cycle race is 20 miles long. About how many hours will it take if I cycle at 10 km per hour?

Swap over and take a turn at answering some questions. Discuss the strategies you used to solve the calculations.

Read, choose and use standard metric units

Aim

- To read, choose and use standard metric units to estimate and measure capacity.

Think about and discuss

For the units below, what might measure approximately two of each?

- A kilometre
- A centimetre
- An hour
- A minute
- A metre
- A kilogram
- A millimetre
- A litre

Here is an example: two hours is about the time I spend playing football each week.

I think I can measure this in centimetres.

Tell someone how you would convert 50 mm into metres. Find out if they would use the same method.

Read timetables and times using 24-hour notation

Aim

• To read timetables and times using 24-hour notation.

Greenwich Mean Time (GMT) and all of the world's time is set from Greenwich in London. Countries that are to the east of London are ahead (+) of GMT and countries to the west of London are behind (−) GMT.

Country	+/− GMT
Australia	+10 GMT
Hawaii	−10 GMT
Argentina	−3 GMT
China	+8 GMT
New Zealand	+12 GMT
Japan	+9 GMT
Barbados	−4 GMT

Here is an example: if it is 15:00 (3.00 pm) in London, then it will be 23:00 (11:00 pm) in China.

Think about and discuss

In London the time is 16:30.
What time is it in the countries above?

Think about and discuss

My flight takes 11 hours to get from London to Japan. When I land in Japan it is 07:00 local time. What time did my flight leave London?

Think about and discuss

Why do you think we have different time zones such as those written above?

Read timetables using 24-hour notation

Aim

- To read timetables and times using 24-hour notation.

Think about and discuss

Use the Olympic events timetable below and discuss whether the statements beneath it are accurate.

Event	Start time	Finish time
Marathon	08:00	12:00
Rowing	09:15	11:45
Cycling	12:00	15:25
Tennis	14:30	17:30
Hockey	14:30	17:15
Athletics	14:30	19:30
Sailing	15:00	16:45

- The running event that is the longest is athletics.
- The hockey lasts for 2 hours and 45 minutes.
- The tennis finishes 15 minutes before the end of the hockey.
- The cycling finishes one hour after the tennis starts.
- If the cycling starts half an hour early, you could also see the start of the sailing.
- Three events last between two and three hours.

Make up some statements of your own for someone to check.

Tell someone why we use 24-hour time.

Handling data

Interpret line graphs that represent changes over time

Aim

- To interpret line graphs that represent changes over time.

The table below shows one runner's information about a cross-country race

Time (hours)	Distance (miles)
0	0
0.5	4
1.0	7
1.5	10
2.0	14
2.5	16

Tell someone what this data would look like if it was plotted onto a line graph.

Think about and discuss

What happens to the runner's speed through the race? How might you explain this?

Describe and interpret results using the median, mode and mean

Aim

- To describe and interpret results and solutions to problems using the mode, range, median and mean.

- Mean = the average
- Median = the middle number in the order
- Mode = the number which occurs most often
- Range = the difference between the largest and the smallest numbers

Tell someone how you would find the range, mode, median and mean of the amount Charlie saved over seven months, using the table below.

Month	Amount saved
January	£6.00
February	£3.00
March	£4.00
April	£8.00
May	£5.00
June	£12.00
July	£4.00

Think about and discuss

Approximately how much will Charlie save by the end of the year?

Describe and interpret results and solutions to problems

Aim

- To describe and interpret results and solutions to problems.

The table below shows information about the fastest sprinters ever recorded

Surname	Time (secs)	Country	Date
Bolt	9.58	JAM	2008
Gay	9.69	USA	2008
Bailey	9.84	CAN	1996
Gatlin	9.85	USA	2004
Greene	9.87	USA	2000
Lewis	9.92	USA	1988
Christie	9.96	GBR	1992
Lewis	9.99	USA	1984
Crawford	10.06	TRI	1976
Borzov	10.14	URS	1972

Tell someone what the longest time was between world records. Tell them what the smallest margin is by which a runner has made a new world record.

Think about and discuss

Make up some questions of your own to ask someone.